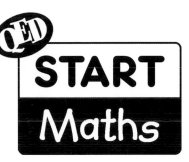

QED
START
Maths

Sizes and Shapes
Book 2

Ann Montague-Smith

QED Publishing

Copyright © QED Publishing 2004

First published in the UK in 2004 by
QED Publishing
A division of Quarto Publishing plc
The Fitzpatrick Building
188-194 York Way, London N7 9QP

A Catalogue record for this book is available from the British Library.

ISBN 1-84538-030-4

Written by Ann Montague-Smith
Designed and edited by The Complete Works
Illustrated by Jenny Tulip
Photography by Steve Lumb and Michael Wicks

Creative Director Louise Morley
Editorial Manager Jean Coppendale

Printed and bound in China

With thanks to:

Contents

Sorting solid shapes

Look at the shapes in the picture.
Name them.

sphere

cone

Point to a shape which is not a cone.

4

cube

pyramid

Challenge
Use a set of shapes to make a model.
Can you name the shapes that you have used?

Building with solid shapes

Look at the picture.
Name the shapes.

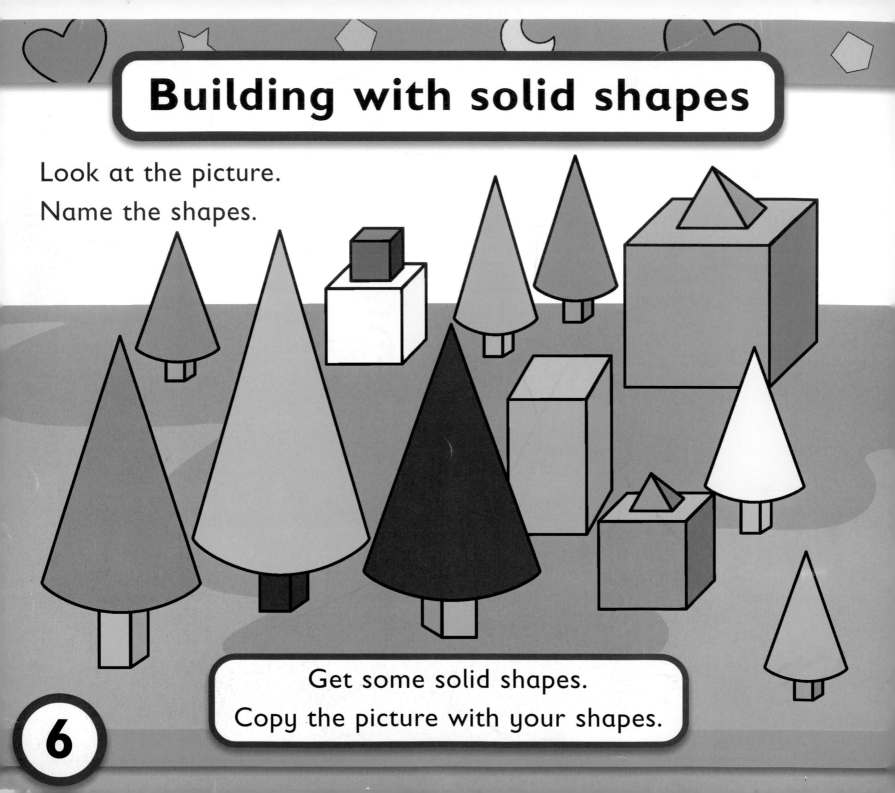

Get some solid shapes.
Copy the picture with your shapes.

6

7

Sorting flat shapes

Look at the shapes in the picture.
Name them.

square   **rectangle**

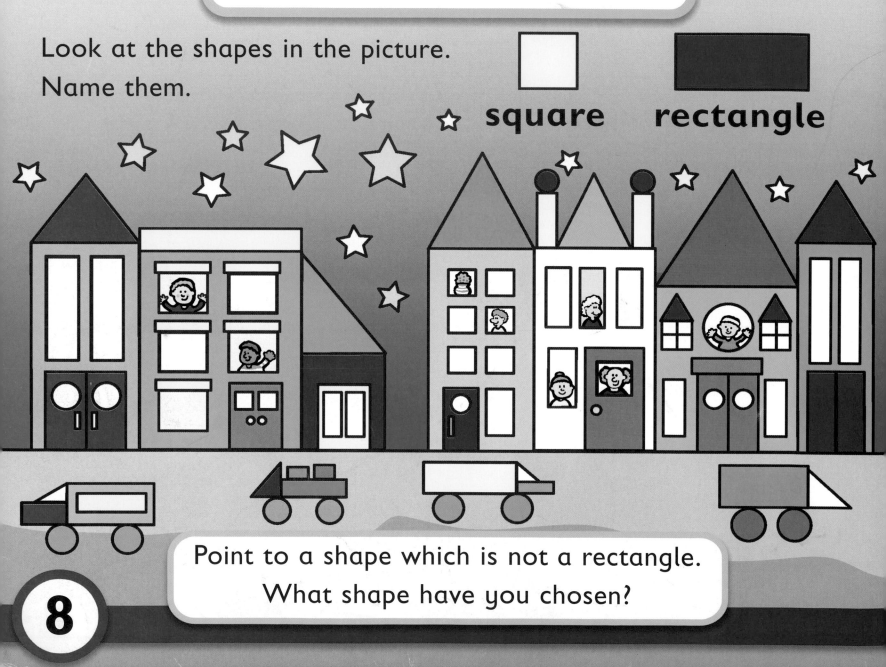

Point to a shape which is not a rectangle.
What shape have you chosen?

circle

triangle

star

Challenge

Look around the room.
Can you find these shapes
in things in the room?

9

Pictures with flat shapes

Get some flat shapes.

Copy the picture with the shapes.

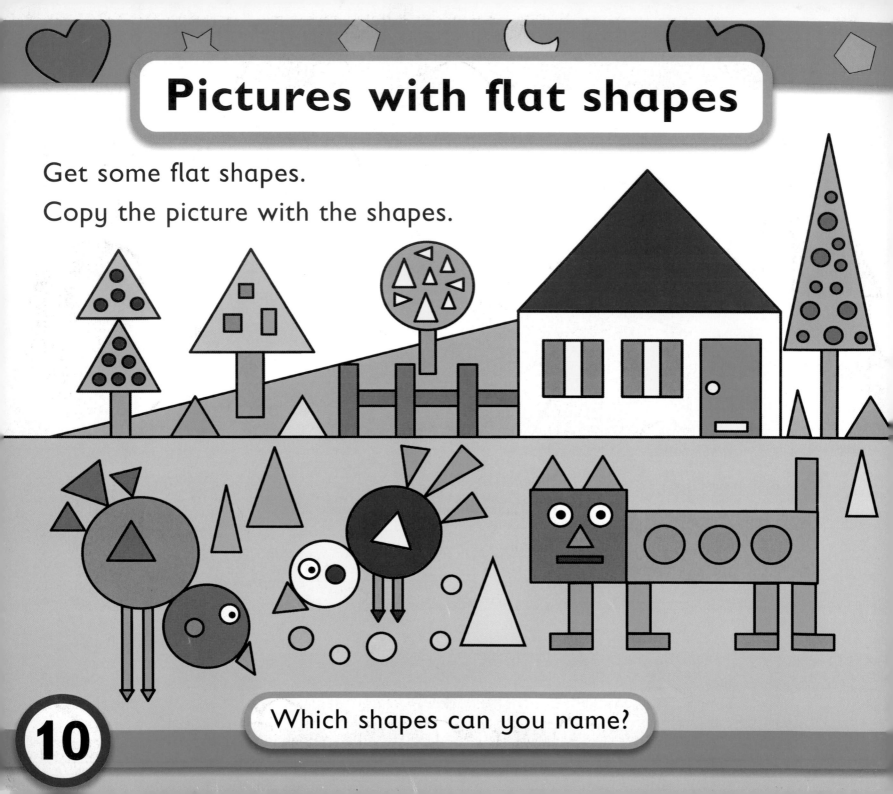

Which shapes can you name?

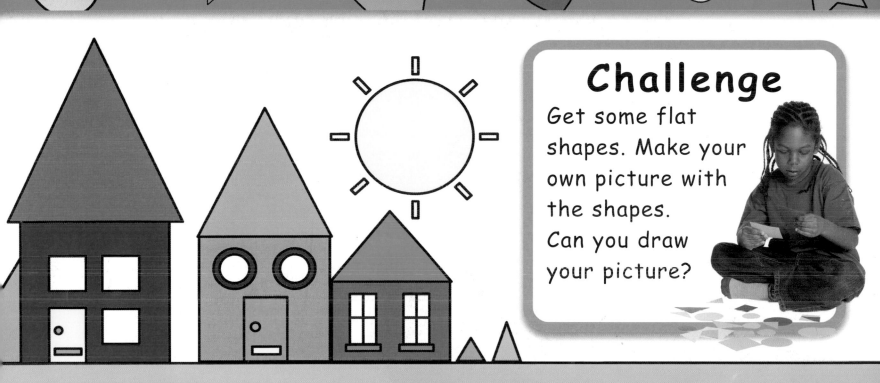

Challenge

Get some flat shapes. Make your own picture with the shapes. Can you draw your picture?

Matching solid shapes

Which shape made each print?

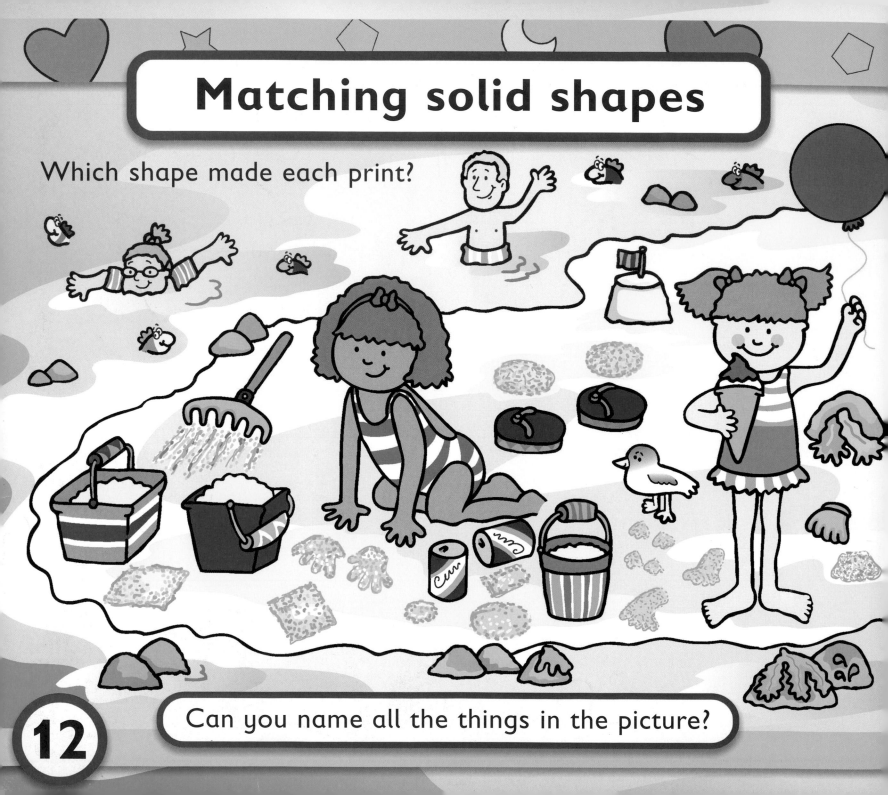

Can you name all the things in the picture?

Challenge

Get some damp sand.
Find some solid shapes.
Look carefully at the faces
of the shapes.
Decide what print it will make.
Now print in the sand.

Making patterns

Say the patterns in each row.

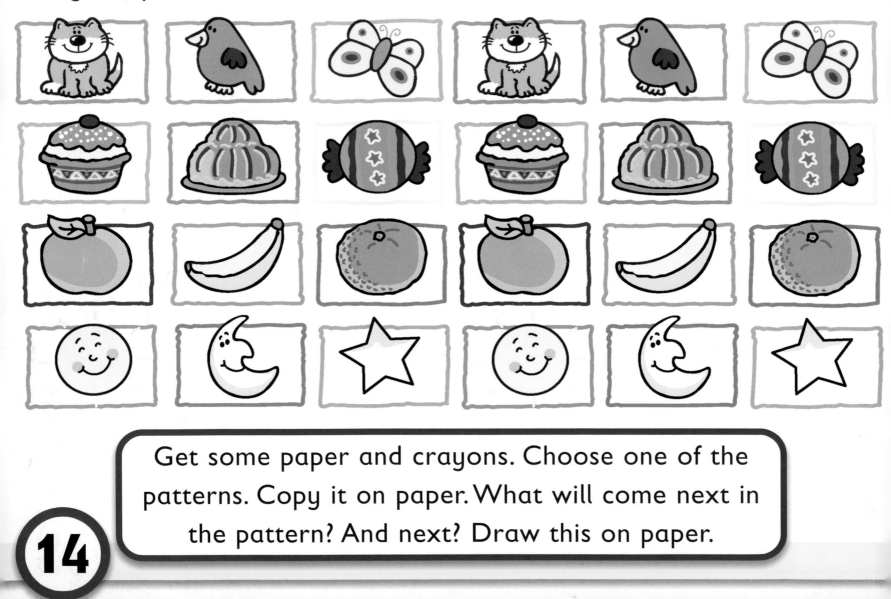

Get some paper and crayons. Choose one of the patterns. Copy it on paper. What will come next in the pattern? And next? Draw this on paper.

Challenge

Get some shape cut-outs.
Make your own pattern.
Say your pattern to a friend.
Can your friend say what will
come next? Now swap over.

Symmetry

Get a small safety mirror.

Put the mirror on the centre line of the cat.

Look in the mirror. What can you see?

Now try the other pictures.

centre

Use the mirror. Put it on the pictures like this. What can you see in the mirror?

Challenge
Fold a sheet of paper in half. Draw a shape and cut it out. Be careful not to cut away the fold. What do you think you will see when you open the paper?

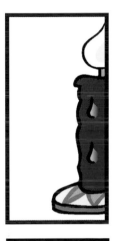

Position

Who is sitting under the table?
What can you see on top of the table?

Where is the ball?
What can you see on the shelf?

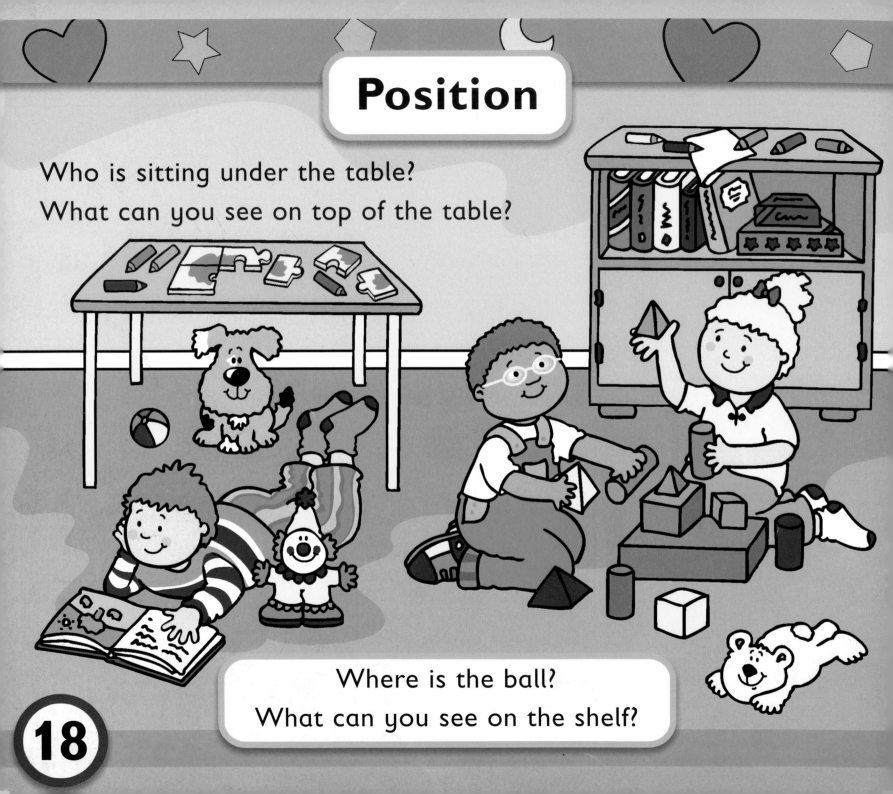

Challenge

Paint a picture of you.
Now paint a cat next to you.
What else would you like in
your picture?

19

Direction and movement

Help the animals to get home.

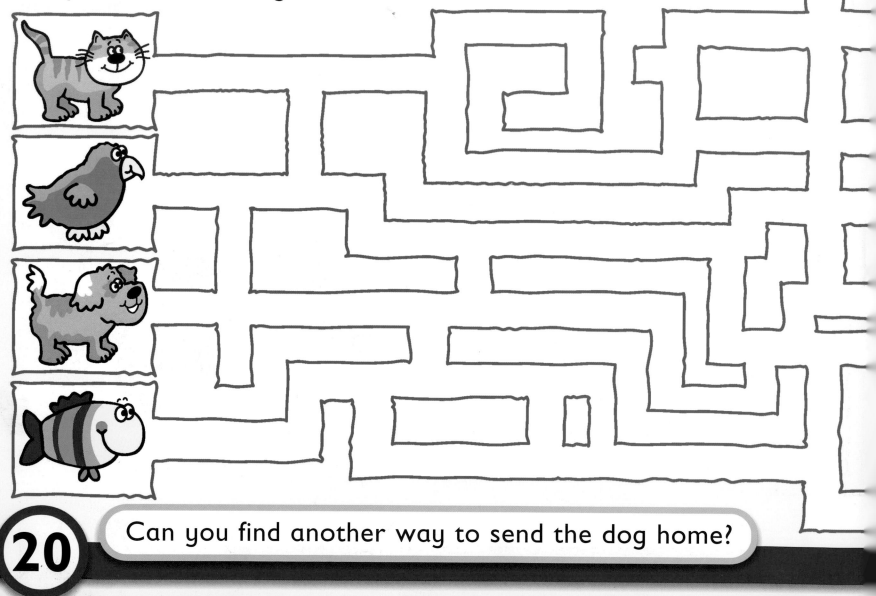

Can you find another way to send the dog home?

Challenge

Find some things in the
room that turn.

Supporting notes for adults

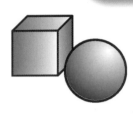

Sorting solid shapes – pages 4-5

Read the shape labels to the children as they point to the mathematical shapes at the top of the pages. Encourage them to find examples of each shape, in turn, in the picture.

Building with solid shapes – pages 6-7

If the children find it difficult to make the shapes in the picture, start with the house. Ask the children to match the shapes to the house, then to build it. They will need a cube and a pyramid for this.

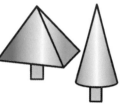

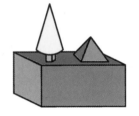

Sorting flat shapes – pages 8-9

Encourage the children to say the name of each shape as you read the label and to point to the mathematical shapes at the top of the pages. Encourage them to find each shape in turn, in the picture.

Pictures with flat shapes – pages 10-11

Ask the children to make each item in the picture. Encourage them to find the shape tiles they will need, and to name these before they begin to make their picture.

22

Matching solid shapes – pages 12-13

The picture includes some everyday items as well as mathematical shapes. Begin with the shell, the footprints… and discuss what could have made these imprints before looking at the mathematical shapes and their imprints.

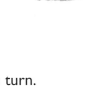

Making patterns – pages 14-15

Ask the children to say what the images are in each sequence such as cat, bird, butterfly, cat, bird, butterfly. Encourage them to repeat this as you point to each image in turn.

Symmetry – pages 16-17

Encourage the children to make a guess of what the whole picture will be before they check with the mirror.

Position – pages 18-19

Ask the children questions such as, 'What is on top… under… beside the…?'

Direction and movement – pages 20-21

Encourage the children to talk about the route that they have chosen and to describe the directions. At this stage they will probably find 'left' and 'right' difficult to remember, so help them by supplying the correct word and pointing along the line of movement on the maze.

Suggestions for using this book

Children will enjoy looking through the book and talking about the colourful pictures. Sit somewhere comfortable together. Please read the instructions to the children, then encourage them to take part in the activity and check whether or not they have understood what to do.

The activities encourage children to use the shapes to make buildings, patterns and pictures so that they learn more about the properties of the shapes. Encourage them to talk about what they have done, what has worked well in their model or picture, and why, and how it could be improved. In this way, they will extend their understanding of the properties of the shapes.

The connection between solid shapes and flat ones is very important for children to understand. Do encourage children to make prints from solid shapes and to describe what they can see. For example, pressing one face of a box into damp sand will leave a rectangular imprint. Now ask the children to describe and name that face of the box.

Children are introduced to the idea of symmetry. It is really useful to have a mirror handy for these activities. Show the children how to place the mirror along the mirror line of the picture and then to see the reflection in the mirror and how it joins to the picture on the page.

Help the children to extend their understanding of the vocabulary for position, direction and movement, by playing 'I Spy', for where things are, and 'Simon Says', for children moving themselves. They will show you by their responses whether or not they understand the vocabulary used.